Comprehension Activities in Poetry: Grad

Table of Contents

Comprehension Activities in Poetry: Grade Two

Introduction

This book is designed to help students become better readers through the reading of poetry. The IRA/NCTE Standards for the English Language Arts list as their first recommendation: "Students read a wide range of print and nonprint texts to build an understanding of texts, of themselves, and of the cultures of the United States and the world...." Poetry is a form of literature easily read and enjoyed by young students. First books often use the rhythm and rhyme of poetry to engage young readers. Because poetry often uses figurative speech, it encourages imagination and creative thinking. As students progress, their enjoyment of poetry grows to encompass different forms and styles. Most students not only enjoy the reading of poetry, but they will also enjoy creating their own verse, both in the school setting and on their own. It is recommended that students encounter a variety of reading selections to hold their interest. Poetry should be included at every grade level.

Because of its language, poetry often lends itself to individual interpretation. However, for the young reader, poetry is more often fun and straightforward. Students' comprehension of the reading of poetry can be tested through questions designed to encourage them to think about their reading. The questions in this book test students' comprehension on six levels: finding the facts, detecting a sequence, learning new vocabulary through context, identifying the main idea, drawing conclusions, and making inferences. Strengthening these skills through the reading of poetry will also aid students in other reading experiences.

Organization

The poems in this book are divided into thematic units to help the teacher to integrate the poetry into other areas of study. The units are Fun and Wonder, All About Me, Different Seasons, and Outside My Window. All of the units include the six comprehension skills listed previously. Each poem is followed by six comprehension questions, always in the same order. The questions increase in difficulty from literal understanding of the text to more complex thinking and reasoning skills. The order of the questions and a brief description of the skills follow:

- **Facts:** The first question focuses on literal comprehension. Students identify pieces of factual information. They look for specific details that tell who, what, when, where, and how.

- **Sequence:** The second question refers to sequence. Students practice identifying the order of events or the steps in a process.

- **Context:** The third question requires students to practice using all the words in the poem to understand unfamiliar words. Students become aware of the relationships between words, phrases, and sentences. Mastering the use of context enables students to become independent readers.

- **Main Idea:** The fourth question deals with the main idea of the poem. Students will identify the overall point made in the poem. Students must be able to differentiate between the main idea and the details that support it.

- **Conclusion:** The fifth question requires students to draw conclusions. Conclusions are not stated in the reading but must be formulated by the students. Students must draw conclusions based only on the information in the poem. They must put together the details from the information as if they were clues to a puzzle. The conclusion students draw must be supported by the details in the poem.

- **Inference:** The sixth question asks students to make inferences. Students make inferences by combining their own knowledge and experiences with what they read. They put together the facts in the poem with what they already know to make a reasonable inference about something that is not stated in the poem. Making inferences requires students to go beyond the information in the poem.

Along with the six questions, each poem is followed by an extension activity related to poetry or the specific poem. The extension activities are designed to further students' appreciation and understanding of reading and writing poetry.

The assessment at the beginning of the book can be used as a pretest to gauge students' reading comprehension skills. It can also be used as a posttest to determine improvements in reading comprehension skills when students have completed the exercises.

Use

The activities in this book are designed for independent use by students who have had instruction in the specific skills covered in the lessons. This book should serve as additional practice with reading comprehension skills. Copies of the activity sheets can be given to individuals or pairs of students for completion. The poems and activities can be used as a center activity. When students are familiar with the content of the worksheets, they can be assigned as homework.

To begin, determine the implementation that fits your students' needs and your classroom structure. The following plan suggests a format for this implementation.

1. Administer the assessment to establish baseline information on each student. This test may also be used as a posttest when the student has completed the book.

2. Explain the purpose of the worksheets to the class.

3. Review the mechanics of how you want students to work with the activities. Do you want them to work in pairs? Are the activities for homework?

4. Introduce students to the process and purpose of the activities. Work with students when they have difficulty. Give them only one poem at a time to avoid pressure.

5. Read a poem together. Review with the students each comprehension skill by using the poem's activities as a practice example. Read through the extension activity together.

Integrating Poetry into the Curriculum

Improving reading comprehension skills in language arts has obvious merits for other areas of study as well. Reading and writing skills are important in all curriculum areas, and language arts are naturally integrated into all subject areas through vocabulary, descriptions, reading directions, and answering questions.

Poetry is a form of literature that can be easily brought into other curriculum areas through subject matter. Poems about nature and animals go hand-in-hand with science studies. Poems concerning people and places complement social studies. Poems about numbers and sequence can bring literature to math class. The rhythm and rhyme of poems have always been a part of music, dance, and games. The descriptive language of poetry lends itself to artwork and imagination. The fun and pleasure of poetry can be used to enrich learning across the curriculum.

Poetry and the 4-Blocks Model

The 4-Blocks Model for teaching is based on the premise that there are four basic approaches to teaching reading. Students are exposed to all four approaches each day. Each block has something different to offer each student, and no student is left out of the learning process. Though the model was designed for younger grades, specifically first and second, adaptations can be applied to make it work at higher levels. The four blocks are Guided Reading, Self-Selected Reading, Working with Words, and Writing. Although each block must be taught each day, and a pre-subscribed amount of time allotted to each block, teachers may decide when each block best fits into his or her class time. In other words, there is no correct order in which to teach the blocks.

The purpose of the **Guided Reading** block is to expose students to many different types of print. The teacher may begin the block by discussing the topic of the reading selection. He or she may provide necessary background information. This block focuses on comprehension skills. Since rereading and understanding are the focus, this format works well for introducing poetry.

The **Self-Selected Reading** block may begin with a teacher reading. Then students choose books that they want to read. To encourage familiarity with poetry, many different books of verse and poems should be available to choose from.

The **Working with Words** block helps children to remember frequently misspelled words and high-frequency words. It includes a "word wall" where the words are easily accessible. The block focuses on spelling strategies and writing skills as opposed to vocabulary and reading skills. High-frequency and frequently misspelled words from the poems would be included on the word wall.

The **Writing** block concentrates on all aspects of writing. The teacher discusses the habits of good writers, editing techniques, inventive spelling, illustrating, and beginning and ending stories. The students choose their best writing for publishing and sharing. Poetry could easily be incorporated into the writing block.

The 4-Blocks Model has proved to be a successful tool for teaching reading and writing skills in many schools across the nation. It is naturally more complex than the brief summary given here. More information on the 4-Blocks Model can be found at **http://www.teachers.net.**

Foreign Lands

by Robert Louis Stevenson

Up into the cherry tree
Who should climb but little me?
I held the trunk with both my hands
And looked abroad in foreign lands.

I saw the next door garden lie,
Adorned with flowers, before my eye,
And many pleasant places more
That I had never seen before.

I saw the dimpling river pass
And be the sky's blue looking-glass;
The dusty roads go up and down
With people tramping in to town.

If I could find a higher tree
Farther and farther I should see,
To where the grown-up river slips
Into the sea among the ships,

To where the road on either hand
Leads onward into fairy land,
Where all the children dine at five,
And all the playthings come alive.

Go on to the next page.

Foreign Lands, p. 2

DIRECTIONS Think about the poem. Then answer these questions. Fill in the circle before the correct answer.

1. Where is the person in the poem?

   Ⓐ on a rooftop
   Ⓑ in a tree
   Ⓒ on a river

2. What does he do after he climbs the tree?

   Ⓐ picks cherries
   Ⓑ climbs a higher tree
   Ⓒ looks all around

3. People "tramping" in to town are

   Ⓐ walking.
   Ⓑ riding.
   Ⓒ driving.

4. This poem is mostly about

   Ⓐ a cherry tree.
   Ⓑ a fairy land.
   Ⓒ seeing new things.

5. What the person in the poem sees is new to him because

   Ⓐ he has never been so high up.
   Ⓑ he has never looked around.
   Ⓒ he has never climbed a tree.

6. You can tell that the person in the poem

   Ⓐ likes to imagine things.
   Ⓑ is afraid to climb high.
   Ⓒ does not care for cherries.

I Saw A Ship A-Sailing

by Mother Goose

I saw a ship a-sailing,
A-sailing on the sea;
And, oh! it was all laden
With pretty things for thee!

There were candies in the cabin,
And apples in the hold;
The sails were made of silk,
And the masts were made of gold.

The four-and-twenty sailors
That stood between the decks,
Were four-and-twenty white mice
With chains about their necks.

The captain was a duck,
With a packet on his back;
And when the ship began to move,
The captain said, "Quack! Quack!"

Go on to the next page.

I Saw A Ship A-Sailing, p. 2

 **DIRECTIONS** **Think about the poem. Then answer these questions. Fill in the circle before the correct answer.**

1. What was made of gold?

    Ⓐ the ship
    Ⓑ the sails
    Ⓒ the masts

2. After the ship began to move,

    Ⓐ the captain said, "Quack! Quack!"
    Ⓑ the sailors became mice.
    Ⓒ the captain saw a duck.

3. The word "laden" means

    Ⓐ sinking.
    Ⓑ floating.
    Ⓒ full.

4. The poem is mostly about

    Ⓐ the sea.
    Ⓑ a duck.
    Ⓒ a ship.

5. The ship is most likely

    Ⓐ not real.
    Ⓑ very old.
    Ⓒ quite small.

6. The poet probably wrote this poem

    Ⓐ for a stranger.
    Ⓑ for someone special.
    Ⓒ for herself.

POETRY PATCH

This poem tells about a beautiful ship. The poet gives many details to tell how the ship looks. Draw a picture of the ship using the details from the poem.

A Good Play

by Robert Louis Stevenson

We built a ship upon the stairs
All made of the back-bedroom chairs,
And filled it full of soft pillows
To go a-sailing on the billows.

We took a saw and several nails,
And water in the nursery pails;
And Tom said, "Let us also take
An apple and a slice of cake;"—
Which was enough for Tom and me
To go a-sailing on, till tea.

We sailed along for days and days,
And had the very best of plays;
But Tom fell out and hurt his knee,
So there was no one left but me.

Go on to the next page.

A Good Play, p. 2

 **Think about the poem. Then answer these questions. Fill in the circle before the correct answer.**

1. Where did the children make the ship?

   Ⓐ in the nursery
   Ⓑ on the stairs
   Ⓒ on the water

2. The children sailed

   Ⓐ after tea.
   Ⓑ during tea.
   Ⓒ before tea.

3. "Billows" probably means

   Ⓐ meadows.
   Ⓑ waves.
   Ⓒ chairs.

4. The poem is mostly about

   Ⓐ children having fun.
   Ⓑ playing with chairs.
   Ⓒ Tom getting hurt.

5. After Tom fell out of the boat,

   Ⓐ he got back in.
   Ⓑ he stopped playing.
   Ⓒ both boys stopped playing.

6. When the poet says they "sailed along for days and days," he means

   Ⓐ that the boys sailed for many days.
   Ⓑ that the boys sailed for one day.
   Ⓒ that the boys pretended to sail for days.

POETRY PATCH

Choose a partner and act out this poem while you say the words. Pretend to build a ship with chairs and pillows. Take turns saying the lines.

Monster Manners

by Thomasin Heyworth

There was a monster in my house,
He was so very rude.
He never said, "Oh, may I please?"
Just ate up all our food!
When he smashed up all my things,
I walked him to the door,
Said, "Mr. Monster, learn your manners, please,
Or don't come back anymore!"

Go on to the next page.

Monster Manners, p. 2

DIRECTIONS **Think about the poem. Then answer these questions. Fill in the circle before the correct answer.**

1. What did the monster need?

Ⓐ food
Ⓑ friends
Ⓒ manners

2. Which thing happened first?

Ⓐ The monster had to leave.
Ⓑ The monster ate all the food.
Ⓒ The monster smashed things.

3. "Rude" means

Ⓐ not polite.
Ⓑ not pretty.
Ⓒ not fun.

POETRY PATCH

4. The poet wants people to

Ⓐ invite monsters to their homes.
Ⓑ use good manners.
Ⓒ smash other people's things.

5. The poet made the monster

Ⓐ leave the house.
Ⓑ stay longer.
Ⓒ learn some manners.

6. If the monster becomes polite,

Ⓐ he must stay away.
Ⓑ he may visit other monsters.
Ⓒ he may come back to visit the poet.

As a class, make a list of good manners to use at school. Try using perfect manners for one week. Divide the class into teams. Give each team 20 points. Each time a student forgets to use good manners, a point is taken away from his or her team. At the end of a week, the team with the most points left has the winning manners!

Simple Simon

by Mother Goose

Simple Simon met a pieman,
Going to the fair;
Said Simple Simon to
    the pieman,
"Let me taste your ware."

Said the pieman to
    Simple Simon,
"Show me first your penny."
Said Simple Simon to
    the pieman,
"Indeed, I have not any."

Simple Simon went a-fishing
For to catch a whale;
All the water he could find
Was in his mother's pail!

Simple Simon went to look
If plums grew on a thistle;
He pricked his fingers
    very much,
Which made poor
    Simon whistle.

He went to catch a dicky bird
And thought he could not fail,
Because he had a little salt
To put upon its tail.

He went for water with
    a sieve,
But soon it ran all through;
And now poor Simple Simon
Bids you all adieu.

Go on to the next page.

Simple Simon, p. 2

 **Think about the poem. Then answer these questions. Fill in the circle before the correct answer.**

1. How did Simon plan to catch a bird?

Ⓐ by using a sieve
Ⓑ with water from a pail
Ⓒ by putting salt on its tail

2. After Simon tried to catch the bird,

Ⓐ he went to get water with a sieve.
Ⓑ he went fishing for a whale.
Ⓒ he met the pieman.

3. The pieman's "ware" is

Ⓐ pie.
Ⓑ where he is.
Ⓒ his cart.

4. The poem is mostly about

Ⓐ how Simon fishes.
Ⓑ Simon's troubles.
Ⓒ how to catch a bird.

5. What word best tells about Simon?

Ⓐ brave
Ⓑ foolish
Ⓒ clever

6. The next time Simon does something, he is mostly likely to

Ⓐ make a mistake.
Ⓑ do it well.
Ⓒ ask for help.

POETRY PATCH

Many poems use rhyming words. Words that rhyme sound alike, such as "nose" and "toes." Make a list of the rhyming words in "Simple Simon." You should find seven rhyming pairs. Then try to think of more words to rhyme with the words in your list. How many did you write?

Treasure

by Hilda Conkling

Robbers carry a treasure
Into a field of wheat.
With a great bag of silk
They go on careful feet.
They dig a hole, deep, deep,
They bury it under a stone,
Cover it up with turf,
Leave it alone.
What is there in the bag?
Stones that shine, gold?
I cannot rob the robbers!
THEY have not told.
Tonight I'd like to know
If they will go
Softly to find the treasure?
I'd like to know
How much yellow gold
A bag like that can hold?

Go on to the next page.

Treasure, p. 2

 **DIRECTIONS** **Think about the poem. Then answer these questions. Fill in the circle before the correct answer.**

1. What were the robbers burying?

Ⓒ an iron box
Ⓑ a silk bag
Ⓒ a treasure chest

2. What do the robbers do first?

Ⓐ dig a deep hole
Ⓑ bury it under a stone
Ⓒ carry it into a field

3. "Turf" is most likely

Ⓐ earth.
Ⓑ cloth.
Ⓒ leaves.

4. What does the poet want to know?

Ⓐ what is in the bag
Ⓑ who the robbers are
Ⓒ where the treasure is

5. The poet thinks the bag is full of gold because

Ⓐ the bag looks heavy.
Ⓑ she saw something shiny.
Ⓒ the robbers are hiding it.

6. The poet is

Ⓐ bored.
Ⓑ happy.
Ⓒ curious.

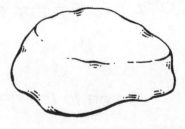

POETRY PATCH

What do you think is in the bag? Write more lines for this poem.
Tell what is in the bag. Tell what you think the robbers do next.

The Swing

by Robert Louis Stevenson

How do you like to go up in a swing,
    Up in the air so blue?
Oh, I do think it the pleasantest thing
    Ever a child can do!

Up in the air and over the wall,
    Till I can see so wide,
River and trees and cattle and all
    Over the countryside—

Till I look down on the garden green,
    Down on the roof so brown—
Up in the air I go flying again,
    Up in the air and down!

Go on to the next page.

The Swing, p. 2

 **DIRECTIONS** **Think about the poem. Then answer these questions. Fill in the circle before the correct answer.**

1. What does the poet like best?

- Ⓐ flying
- Ⓑ cows
- Ⓒ swinging

2. When the poet swings high,

- Ⓐ he can touch the sky.
- Ⓑ he feels afraid.
- Ⓒ he can see the countryside.

3. By "pleasantest" the poet means

- Ⓐ most daring.
- Ⓑ most pleasing.
- Ⓒ most simple.

4. The poem is mostly about

- Ⓐ a child on a swing.
- Ⓑ a brown rooftop.
- Ⓒ cows in a field.

5. The poet is most likely

- Ⓐ an old man.
- Ⓑ a young woman.
- Ⓒ a little boy.

6. The poet has probably

- Ⓐ never been on a swing.
- Ⓑ only heard of swinging.
- Ⓒ done a lot of swinging.

POETRY PATCH

How do you feel about swinging? Write your own poem about swinging. Use some rhyming words.

All of Me

by Thomasin Heyworth

I, myself, and me
Climbed into a big oak tree.
I wanted to get down
And walk around.
Me wanted to stay
In the tree.
Myself was hungry,
And wanted a snack,
So we said,
"Let's do all three!"

Go on to the next page.

All of Me, p. 2

 **DIRECTIONS** Think about the poem. Then answer these questions. Fill in the circle before the correct answer.

1. I, myself, and me

Ⓐ decide to stay in the tree.
Ⓑ decide to walk around.
Ⓒ decide to do three things.

2. After climbing the tree,

Ⓐ the poet gets hungry.
Ⓑ the poet finds a friend.
Ⓒ the poet wants to climb higher.

3. In the poem, "we" means

Ⓐ many children.
Ⓑ the tree and the poet.
Ⓒ I, myself, and me.

4. This poem is about

Ⓐ one person
Ⓑ three people.
Ⓒ an oak tree.

5. I, myself, and me can agree because

Ⓐ they are good friends.
Ⓑ they are the same person.
Ⓒ they are nice people.

6. You can tell that the poet

Ⓐ is happy playing alone.
Ⓑ wishes for friends.
Ⓒ climbs many trees.

POETRY PATCH

Write a "name poem" about yourself! Write the first letter of your name at the top left-hand side of your paper. Write the second letter of your name below the first letter. Keep writing the rest of your name down the side of the paper. Then write a word that tells about you for each letter in your name. Here is an example. If the first letter of your name is "F," you might write the word "Fun."

I'd Like to Be an Engineer

by Brenda Lavigne

I'd like to be an engineer.
I think I really could.
I like my math and science;
At these, I'm very good!

I like to take things all apart,
To see what makes them go.
People say that I am smart—
I build them back just so!

My mother calls me curious.
My father calls me "Doc."
My brother is just furious—
(I took apart his clock).

I have it back together now,
And it is working fine.
My brother won't admit it,
But it's telling better time!

Go on to the next page.

Name _____   Date _____

I'd Like to Be an Engineer, p. 2

 **DIRECTIONS** Think about the poem. Then answer these questions. Fill in the circle before the correct answer.

1. The poet says she is good at

  Ⓐ reading and writing.
  Ⓑ math and science.
  Ⓒ being an engineer.

2. After she put the clock back together,

  Ⓐ it did not work anymore.
  Ⓑ it kept better time.
  Ⓒ her brother gave it to her.

3. Another word for "furious" is

  Ⓐ worried.
  Ⓑ careful.
  Ⓒ angry.

4. The poet wants readers to know that

  Ⓐ she would be a good engineer.
  Ⓑ people think she is smart.
  Ⓒ she can fix clocks.

5. The poet's brother won't say his clock works better because

  Ⓐ he could not fix it.
  Ⓑ he would have to say his sister is smart.
  Ⓒ he cannot tell time.

6. If the poet had a music box, she would probably most enjoy

  Ⓐ listening to the music.
  Ⓑ looking at it.
  Ⓒ seeing how it worked.

POETRY PATCH

Part of a poem's sound is its meter. Meter is a rhythm. It has a pattern. See what the meter is for this poem. As you read each line, make a mark for each syllable you hear. Then count your marks. For example, the first line has eight syllables: I'd/like/to/be/an/en/gi/neer. Write the number 8 next to that line. When you have counted all the lines, look at your numbers. Do you see a pattern?

Growing

by Thomasin Heyworth

Whose clothes are these
I'm trying to wear
With sleeves so short
And legs up to there?
I can't venture out
With my tummy showing—
These clothes are MINE?
I must be growing!

Go on to the next page.

Growing, p. 2

 **DIRECTIONS** ▶ **Think about the poem. Then answer these questions. Fill in the circle before the correct answer.**

1. What is the poet's problem?

   Ⓐ She cannot find her clothes.
   Ⓑ She does not like her clothes.
   Ⓒ She cannot fit into her clothes.

2. After putting on her clothes, the poet sees

   Ⓐ that they are too small.
   Ⓑ that they do not go together.
   Ⓒ that it is time to go outside.

3. In this poem, "venture" probably means

   Ⓐ adventure.
   Ⓑ go.
   Ⓒ sneak.

4. The poem is mostly about

   Ⓐ new clothes.
   Ⓑ going out.
   Ⓒ growing up.

5. The poet's tummy shows because

   Ⓐ her shirt is too small.
   Ⓑ she is wearing someone else's shirt.
   Ⓒ her shirt has no buttons.

6. The poet is probably surprised because

   Ⓐ she had not noticed that she was growing.
   Ⓑ she did not know that she would grow.
   Ⓒ she does not believe that she is growing.

◖POETRY PATCH◗

Many poems tell how two things are alike or different. This is called compare and contrast. You are growing like the girl in the poem. Look at a picture of yourself when you were two or three years old. Look in a mirror. Write "Same" and "Different" on a piece of paper. Write the ways that you still look the same as you did. Write the ways that you look different.

Bed in Summer

by Robert Louis Stevenson

In winter I get up at night
And dress by yellow candle-light.
In summer quite the other way,
I have to go to bed by day.

I have to go to bed and see
The birds still hopping on the tree,
Or hear the grown-up people's feet
Still going past me in the street.

And does it not seem hard to you,
When all the sky is clear and blue,
And I should like so much to play,
To have to go to bed by day?

Go on to the next page.

Bed in Summer, p. 2

1. The poet does not like

  Ⓐ going to bed with the light on.

  Ⓑ getting up in the winter.

  Ⓒ going to bed when it is light outside.

2. The poet hears people passing in the street

  Ⓐ after he goes to bed.

  Ⓑ while he is sleeping.

  Ⓒ when he wakes.

3. In the poem, "hard" means

  Ⓐ not soft.

  Ⓑ not right.

  Ⓒ not easy.

4. Another name for this poem could be

  Ⓐ "People in the Street."

  Ⓑ "Too Soon for Bed."

  Ⓒ "Candle-Light in Winter."

5. It is light outside at bedtime because

  Ⓐ bedtime is earlier in summer.

  Ⓑ the days are longer in summer.

  Ⓒ the sky is clear and blue.

6. Going to bed in winter is probably

  Ⓐ easier for the poet.

  Ⓑ harder for the poet.

  Ⓒ the same for the poet.

POETRY PATCH

Write a poem about summer. Brainstorm as a class words that make you think of summer. Write the words on the board or on a big piece of paper for the class. Use the words to write your own poem about summer.

Gathering Leaves

by Robert Frost

Spades take up leaves
No better than spoons,
And bags full of leaves
Are light as balloons.

I make a great noise
Of rustling all day
Like rabbit and deer
Running away.

But the mountains I raise
Elude my embrace,
Flowing over my arms
And into my face.

I may load and unload
Again and again
Till I fill the whole shed,
And what have I then?

Next to nothing for weight;
And since they grow duller
From contact with earth,
Next to nothing for color.

Next to nothing for use.
But a crop is a crop,
And who's to say where
The harvest shall stop?

Go on to the next page.

Gathering Leaves, p. 2

 **Think about the poem. Then answer these questions. Fill in the circle before the correct answer.**

1. The poet says the bags of leaves are like

   Ⓐ balloons.
   Ⓑ rabbits.
   Ⓒ mountains.

2. The leaves grow duller and lose their color

   Ⓐ while they are in the trees.
   Ⓑ after they are in the shed.
   Ⓒ while they are on the ground.

3. The poet writes, "But the mountains I raise elude my embrace." He is saying

   Ⓐ he cannot hold onto them.
   Ⓑ he has no room for them.
   Ⓒ he does not want them.

4. This poem is all about

   Ⓐ leaves.
   Ⓑ animals.
   Ⓒ balloons.

5. The poet says, "Spades take up leaves no better than spoons." What does he mean?

   Ⓐ He has no spoons to use.
   Ⓑ The leaves will not stay on either one.
   Ⓒ He has tried to use spoons and spades.

6. The poet would probably agree that gathering leaves

   Ⓐ is important.
   Ⓑ is fun.
   Ⓒ is a waste of time.

POETRY PATCH

Poems use many words that describe. They tell how things look, feel, taste, sound, and smell. Gather some leaves from outdoors. Write as many words as you can to tell about the leaves. See if a classmate can guess what you have described.

Bluebird

by Hilda Conkling

Oh bluebird with light red breast,
And your blue back like a feathered sky,
You have to go down south
Before biting winter comes
And my flower-beds are covered
    with fluff out of the clouds.
Before you go,
Sing me one more song
Of tree-tops down south,
Of mothers singing their babies to sleep,
Of sand and glittering stones
Where rivers pass;
Then . . . good-by!

Go on to the next page.

Name _____ Date _____

Bluebird, p. 2

1. What does the poet want the bird to do?

Ⓐ fly away
Ⓑ sing one more song
Ⓒ look at the flowers

2. The bird will fly south

Ⓐ before singing.
Ⓑ before the summer.
Ⓒ before the winter.

3. Which word means the same as "glittering"?

Ⓐ sparkling
Ⓑ glowing
Ⓒ rolling

4. This poem is mostly about

Ⓐ rivers.
Ⓑ a bird.
Ⓒ going south.

5. What season is it in the poem?

Ⓐ winter
Ⓑ spring
Ⓒ fall

6. The bluebird needs to go south

Ⓐ to stay warm.
Ⓑ to sing its songs.
Ⓒ to find the flower-beds.

POETRY PATCH

In "Bluebird," the bird's back is "like a feathered sky." This means that it is blue like the sky, and it has feathers. It is a pretty way to say that the bird's feathers are blue. Think of an animal that you like. Think of ways that you can describe the animal by comparing it to other things. Here is an example: "My cat's fur is as yellow as the Sun."

The Hayloft

by Robert Louis Stevenson

Through all the pleasant meadow-side
    The grass grew shoulder-high,
Till the shining scythes went far and wide
    And cut it down to dry.

Those green and sweetly smelling crops
    They led the wagons home;
And they piled them here in mountaintops
    For mountaineers to roam.

Here is Mount Clear, Mount Rusty-Nail,
    Mount Eagle and Mount High;—
The mice that in these mountains dwell,
    No happier are than I!

Oh, what a joy to clamber there,
    Oh, what a place for play,
With the sweet, the dim, the dusty air,
    The happy hills of hay!

Go on to the next page.

The Hayloft, p. 2

 **DIRECTIONS** **Think about the poem. Then answer these questions. Fill in the circle before the correct answer.**

1. What is the crop in the poem?

Ⓐ grass
Ⓑ hay
Ⓒ dust

2. Before it was cut down to dry,

Ⓐ the mice played in the hay.
Ⓑ the hay was piled high.
Ⓒ the grass grew shoulder-high.

3. "Scythes" must be

Ⓐ blades.
Ⓑ trucks.
Ⓒ ropes.

4. Another good name for this poem could be

Ⓐ "Mice in Hay."
Ⓑ "Hay Mountains."
Ⓒ "Cutting the Hay."

5. The mountains in the poem are

Ⓐ real mountains.
Ⓑ mounds of hay.
Ⓒ hills of grass.

6. You can tell that the poet

Ⓐ cut the grass himself.
Ⓑ is a mountain-climber.
Ⓒ does not mind the mice.

(POETRY PATCH)

In "The Hayloft," the poet says that one thing is another thing. For example, he does not say the hay is like a mountain. He says the hay is a mountain. Describe something this way. This poem is an example: "My house is a castle./ My chair is a throne./ And I am a princess/ When I am alone!"

Name _____ Date _____

September

by Helen Hunt Jackson

The goldenrod is yellow;
The corn is turning brown;
The trees in apple orchards
With fruit are bending down.

The gentian's bluest fringes
Are curling in the sun;
In dusty pods the milkweed
Its hidden silk has spun.

The sedges flaunt their harvest
In every meadow nook;
And asters by the brook-side
Make asters in the brook.

From dewy lanes at morning
The grapes' sweet odors rise;
At noon the roads all flutter
With yellow butterflies.

By all these lovely tokens
September days are here,
With summer's best of weather,
And autumn's best of cheer.

Go on to the next page.

September, p. 2

 **DIRECTIONS** Think about the poem. Then answer these questions. Fill in the circle before the correct answer.

1. The butterflies in the poem are

    Ⓐ orange.
    Ⓑ blue.
    Ⓒ yellow.

2. In the poem, September is coming

    Ⓐ after summer.
    Ⓑ before summer.
    Ⓒ after winter.

3. "Fringes" are

    Ⓐ edges.
    Ⓑ toes.
    Ⓒ eyelashes.

4. The poem is mostly about

    Ⓐ corn.
    Ⓑ seasons.
    Ⓒ grapes.

5. In the poem, "And asters by the brook-side Make asters in the brook." This means

    Ⓐ the flowers are growing in the water.
    Ⓑ the brook is like a mirror for the flowers.
    Ⓒ the flowers are falling into the water.

6. You can tell that the poet

    Ⓐ does not like autumn.
    Ⓑ lives by a brook.
    Ⓒ enjoys autumn.

POETRY PATCH

The poet has painted a picture with words. She tells how the world looks in September where she lives. Paint a picture to go with the poem. Read the poem again as you paint.

If All the Seas Were One Sea

by Mother Goose

If all the seas were one sea,
What a great sea that would be!
And if all the trees were one tree,
What a great tree that would be!
And if all the axes were one axe,
What a great axe that would be!
And if all the men were one man,
What a great man he would be!
And if the great man took the great axe,
And cut down the great tree,
And let it fall into the great sea,
What a splish splash that would be!

Go on to the next page.

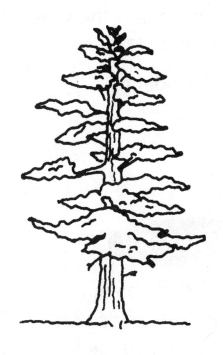

Name _____   Date _____

If All the Seas Were One Sea, p. 2

 **DIRECTIONS** **Think about the poem. Then answer these questions. Fill in the circle before the correct answer.**

1. What does the man do with the axe?

ⓐ He throws it into the sea.
ⓑ He makes it bigger.
ⓒ He cuts down the tree.

2. What happens after the tree is cut?

ⓐ It falls into the sea.
ⓑ It becomes a man.
ⓒ It becomes a great tree.

3. In this poem, the word "great" means

ⓐ wonderful.
ⓑ big.
ⓒ famous.

4. The poem is mostly

ⓐ about a great splash.
ⓑ about a great axe.
ⓒ a silly story.

5. The poet is writing about

ⓐ something make-believe.
ⓑ something that happened.
ⓒ something that could happen.

6. If the man in the poem built a house out of the tree, it would most likely

ⓐ be a tall house.
ⓑ be a great house.
ⓒ be a white house.

POETRY PATCH

Think of some more lines that you could add to this poem. What might the man do with the tree? Maybe a fish sees the tree. Perhaps a bird lived in the tree. Use your imagination!

Unit Four: Outside My Window
Poetry 2, SV 2046-X

The Moon

by Robert Louis Stevenson

The Moon has a face like the clock in the hall;
She shines on thieves on the garden wall,
On streets and fields and harbor quays,
And birdies asleep in the forks of the trees.

The squalling cat and the squeaking mouse,
The howling dog by the door of the house,
The bat that lies in bed at noon,
All love to be out by the light of the Moon.

But all of the things that belong to the day
Cuddle to sleep to be out of her way;
And flowers and children close their eyes
Till up in the morning the Sun shall arise.

Go on to the next page.

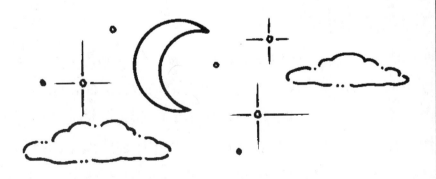

The Moon, p. 2

 **DIRECTIONS**   **Think about the poem. Then answer these questions. Fill in the circle before the correct answer.**

1. Which ones like the light of the Moon?

  Ⓐ children
  Ⓑ flowers
  Ⓒ bats

2. In the poem, flowers close their eyes

  Ⓐ until the Sun rises.
  Ⓑ after the Sun rises.
  Ⓒ until the Moon rises.

3. A "squalling" cat is a

  Ⓐ peaceful cat.
  Ⓑ curious cat.
  Ⓒ noisy cat.

4. This poem tells about

  Ⓐ clocks.
  Ⓑ the Moon.
  Ⓒ sleeping.

5. Flowers and children

  Ⓐ enjoy the light of the Sun.
  Ⓑ like to sleep all day.
  Ⓒ are like cats and mice.

6. The Moon's face is probably like the clock's because

  Ⓐ they both have numbers.
  Ⓑ they are both round.
  Ⓒ they both have hands.

POETRY PATCH

Make a night and day window. You will need construction paper (black and yellow), markers, magazines, glue, a paper punch, and string. Glue the paper together, back to back. Make each side of the paper look like a window with six panes. On the yellow side, draw or glue pictures of things you see in the daytime. On the black side, draw or glue pictures of nighttime things.

Hills

by Hilda Conkling

The hills are going somewhere;
They have been on the way a long time.
They are like camels in a line
But they move more slowly.
Sometimes at sunset they carry silks,
But most of the time silver birch trees,
Heavy rocks, heavy trees, gold leaves
On heavy branches till they are aching . . .
Birches like silver bars they can hardly lift
With grass so thick about their feet to hinder . . .
They have not gone far
In the time I've watched them . . .

Go on to the next page.

Hills, p. 2

DIRECTIONS **Think about the poem. Then answer these questions.
Fill in the circle before the correct answer.**

1. The hills are like which animals?

Ⓐ camels
Ⓑ whales
Ⓒ elephants

2. Since the poet began watching,

Ⓐ the hills have not moved.
Ⓑ the hills have not moved far.
Ⓒ the hills have all changed.

3. Thick grass "hinders" the hills. "Hinders" means

Ⓐ helps.
Ⓑ pushes.
Ⓒ stops.

4. Another title for this poem could be

Ⓐ "Moving Along."
Ⓑ "Heavy Hills."
Ⓒ "The Birches."

5. The hills remind the poet of camels because

Ⓐ they look like camels' humps.
Ⓑ they are brown.
Ⓒ they are in the desert.

6. The poet seems to say that the hills could move more quickly

Ⓐ if they were pushed.
Ⓑ if they were smaller.
Ⓒ if there were not so many heavy things on them.

POETRY PATCH

This poem does not use rhyming words. The poet simply wrote her
thoughts about hills. She made it interesting by using describing
words. She also compared things. Write a poem like this one.
Do not worry about rhyming.

Robin Redbreast

by Mother Goose

Little Robin Redbreast sat upon a tree,
Up went Pussy-Cat, down went he,
Down came Pussy-Cat, away Robin ran,
Says little Robin Redbreast: "Catch me if you can!"

Little Robin Redbreast jumped upon a spade,
Pussy-Cat jumped after him, and then he was afraid.
Little Robin chirped and sang, and what did Pussy say?
Pussy-Cat said: "Mew, mew, mew," and Robin flew away.

Go on to the next page.

Robin Redbreast, p. 2

 **DIRECTIONS** **Think about the poem. Then answer these questions. Fill in the circle before the correct answer.**

1. This poem is about a robin and

  Ⓐ a tree.
  Ⓑ a spade.
  Ⓒ a cat.

2. What did the robin do first?

  Ⓐ jumped on a spade
  Ⓑ sat on a tree
  Ⓒ flew away

3. Which two words mean the same thing?

  Ⓐ chirped, sang
  Ⓑ jumped, sat
  Ⓒ afraid, away

4. This poem is mostly about

  Ⓐ two animal friends.
  Ⓑ an animal chase.
  Ⓒ a brave cat.

5. The robin runs from the cat because

  Ⓐ the robin is the cat's friend.
  Ⓑ the cat and the robin are playing.
  Ⓒ the robin is afraid of the cat.

6. The cat probably wants to catch the robin because

  Ⓐ the cat is hungry.
  Ⓑ the robin is pretty.
  Ⓒ the robin can talk.

(POETRY PATCH)

It is fun to remember a poem. Then you can say it whenever you want. Read this poem again. Say it aloud until you can remember it without looking. Remember the name of the poem and the poet's name, too. Share the poem with your family. First, say, "Robin Redbreast, by Mother Goose." Then say the poem.

Only Morning-Glory That Flowered

by Hilda Conkling

Under the vine I saw one morning-glory
A tight unfolding bud
Half out.
He looked hard down into my lettuce-bed.
He was thinking hard.
He said I want a friend!
I was standing there:
I said, Well, I am here! Don't you see me?
But he thought and thought.

The next day I found him happy,
Quite out,
Looking about the world.
The wind blew sweet airs,
Carried away his perfume in the Sun;
And near by swung a new flower
Uncurling its hands . . .
He was not thoughtful
Anymore!

Go on to the next page.

Only Morning-Glory That Flowered, p. 2

 **DIRECTIONS** Think about the poem. Then answer these questions. Fill in the circle before the correct answer.

1. What did the morning-glory want?

   Ⓐ a place to grow
   Ⓑ some water
   Ⓒ a friend

2. After the poet saw the morning-glory,

   Ⓐ it kept on thinking.
   Ⓑ it was happy.
   Ⓒ it looked around.

3. The flower's "perfume" is its

   Ⓐ smell.
   Ⓑ petals.
   Ⓒ color.

POETRY PATCH

4. This poem is mostly about

   Ⓐ growing a garden.
   Ⓑ looking at flowers.
   Ⓒ having a friend.

5. The poet could not help the morning-glory because

   Ⓐ she was not a flower.
   Ⓑ she did not see it.
   Ⓒ she was not there.

6. You can tell that the poet

   Ⓐ is a busy person.
   Ⓑ likes flowers.
   Ⓒ is lonely.

The poet writes about the flower as if it were a person. Are flowers thoughtful? Flowers do not really think. But in the poem, the flower thinks. It has the same feelings that people do. Look at some other poems. Can you find more examples of animals or plants that do things that people do?

The Wind

by Robert Louis Stevenson

I saw you toss the kites on high
And blow the birds about the sky;
And all around I heard you pass,
Like ladies' skirts across the grass—
    O wind, a-blowing all day long,
    O wind, that sings so loud a song!

I saw the different things you did,
But always you yourself you hid.
I felt you push, I heard you call,
I could not see yourself at all—
    O wind, a-blowing all day long,
    O wind, that sings so loud a song!

O you that are so strong and cold,
O blower, are you young or old?
Are you a beast of field and tree,
Or just a stronger child than me?
    O wind, a-blowing all day long,
    O wind, that sings so loud a song!

Go on to the next page.

The Wind, p. 2

 **DIRECTIONS** Think about the poem. Then answer these questions. Fill in the circle before the correct answer.

1. What does the wind toss?

  Ⓐ kites
  Ⓑ skirts
  Ⓒ birds

2. The poet hears the wind, and then

  Ⓐ he sees the wind.
  Ⓑ he looks for the wind.
  Ⓒ he finds the wind.

3. A "beast" is

  Ⓐ a plant.
  Ⓑ a bird.
  Ⓒ an animal.

4. This poem is mostly about

  Ⓐ hiding.
  Ⓑ flying kites.
  Ⓒ the wind.

5. The poet thinks the wind is hiding because

  Ⓐ they are playing a game.
  Ⓑ he cannot see the wind.
  Ⓒ the wind is in the field.

6. The poet thinks that the wind is

  Ⓐ a mystery.
  Ⓑ frightening.
  Ⓒ not interesting.

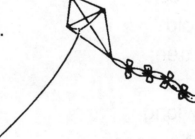

(POETRY PATCH)

We cannot see the wind. But we can see what the wind does. Draw and color a picture showing a windy day. How can you tell that it is windy in your picture?

Comprehension Activities in Poetry: Grade Two

Answer Key

P. 6
Assessment
1. B
2. C
3. A
4. C
5. A
6. A

P. 8
1. C
2. A
3. C
4. C
5. A
6. B

P. 10
1. B
2. C
3. B
4. A
5. B
6. C

P. 12
1. C
2. B
3. A
4. B
5. A
6. C

P. 14
1. C
2. A
3. A
4. B
5. B
6. A

P. 16
1. B
2. C
3. A
4. A
5. C
6. C

P. 18
1. C
2. C
3. B
4. A
5. C
6. C

P. 20
1. C
2. A
3. C
4. A
5. B
6. A

P. 22
1. B
2. B
3. C
4. A
5. B
6. C

P. 24
1. C
2. A
3. B
4. C
5. A
6. A

P. 26
1. C
2. A
3. C
4. B
5. B
6. A

P. 28
1. A
2. C
3. A
4. A
5. B
6. C

P. 30
1. B
2. C
3. A
4. B
5. C
6. A

Poetry 2, SV 2046-X

P. 32
1. B
2. C
3. A
4. B
5. B
6. C

P. 34
1. C
2. A
3. A
4. B
5. B
6. C

P. 36
1. C
2. A
3. B
4. C
5. A
6. B

P. 38
1. C
2. A
3. C
4. B
5. A
6. B

P. 40
1. A
2. B
3. C
4. B
5. A
6. C

P. 42
1. C
2. B
3. A
4. B
5. C
6. A

P. 44
1. C
2. A
3. A
4. C
5. A
6. B

P. 46
1. A
2. B
3. C
4. C
5. B
6. A